Lotty can see a little ship in the water tub next to the shed.

She goes to look at the ship.

She jumps in the tub to get it.

She plays in the water with the ship.

She has fun in the water.

Splash, splash, splash.

Kevin comes to see the ship.

He jumps in the water too.

Oh no!   Smash ... crash ...

The water tub splits.

The water goes all over the path.

Splash, splash, splash.

Bump! Lotty lands on the path.

Splash, splash, splash.

Splash. Kevin lands on the top of Lotty.

Splash, splash, splash.

Oh no! Look at the ship!

Kevin and Lotty are on the top of it.